JB MIDDLETON, C.
Catherine, Duchess of
Cambridge /
Hunter, Nick.
33341005510523

Catherine, DUCHESS of CAMBRIDGE

Nick Hunter

Chicago, Illinois

© 2014 Raintree
an imprint of Capstone Global Library, LLC
Chicago, Illinois

To contact Capstone Global Library please
phone 800-747-4992, or visit our website
www.capstonepub.com

Edited by Nick Hunter, James Benefield, and
Abby Colich
Designed by Philippa Jenkins
Picture research by Ruth Blair
Production by Helen McCreath
Originated by Capstone Global Library Ltd.
Printed in the United States of America in
North Mankato, Minnesota

042014
008162RP

Library of Congress Cataloging-in-
Publication Data
Hunter, Nick.
    Catherine, Duchess of Cambridge / Nick
Hunter.
        pages cm.—(Extraordinary women)
    Includes bibliographical references and
index.
    ISBN 978-1-4109-5942-3 (hbk.)—ISBN
978-1-4109-5950-8 (pbk.) 1. Catherine,
Duchess of Cambridge, 1982—Juvenile
literature. 2. William, Prince, Duke of
Cambridge, 1982—Juvenile literature. 3.
Princesses—Great Britain—Biography—Ju-
venile literature. I. Title.

    DA591.A45W555443 2014
    941.086'12092—dc23
    2013017130

Acknowledgments
We would like to thank the following for
permission to reproduce photographs:
Corbis pp. 11 (© Paul Hilton / Demotix),
15 (© Kerry Taylor Auctions/dpa),
24 (© Mark Makela), 36 (© KIRSTY
WiIGGLESWORTH /PA WIRE/epa); Getty
Images pp. 9 (Middleton Family/Clarence
House), 10 (WPA Pool), 16 (AFP PHOTO/
Michael Dunlea), 17 (Tim Graham), pp. 19,
20 (Mark Cuthbert/UK Press), pp. 25, 42
(Chris Jackson), 27 (Anwar Hussein), 29
(Samir Hussein/WireImage), pp. 30, 35, 43
(Indigo), 40 (Mary Turner - WPA Pool);
Images/PA Wire p. 41; Photoshot pp. 4 (©
CPNA), pp. 5, 28, 31 (© Pool), 6 (© LFI),
7 (© Picture Alliance), 14 (TIPS), 18 (©
UPPA), 22, 23, 33, 37, 38, 39 (© Imago);
Rex Features p. 13; Shutterstock pp. 8 (©
Rossillicon Photos), 12 (© Samot), 21 (©
B747), 26 (© dutourdumonde), 34 (© Gail
Johnson).

CONTENTS

Some words are shown in bold, **like this**. You can find out what they mean by looking in the glossary.

The Big Day

A wedding is one of the most important days in anyone's life. It marks a commitment to share your life with another person. When Catherine Middleton woke up on her wedding day, she knew that her life would never be the same again.

Thousands of people lined the streets and waved British flags to celebrate the royal wedding.

BREAKING BOUNDARIES

MEDIA MADNESS

The royal wedding was a massive **media** event. Two billion people saw the TV pictures and news reports. Facebook chattered with millions of status updates, and there were more than 200 tweets every second about the wedding.

Catherine and William greet the crowds from the balcony of Buckingham Palace.

Catherine's wedding was not held in the local church near her family home in Berkshire, England. Instead, she would travel through huge cheering crowds to Westminster Abbey, the scene of **coronations** and royal weddings for centuries. The **fiancé** she had met as a student was no ordinary young man. Prince William was second in line to the British throne, and one of the world's most famous people.

Royal Future

The wedding would **propel** Catherine into a world of royal privilege and global fame that few people ever experience. She must have wondered how she would cope with the glare of publicity and the royal duties that would dominate her married life.

"Beaming Bride"

The wedding was reported all over the world. The *Washington Post* wrote on 29 April 2011,

"After a majestic wedding in Westminster Abbey ... the lofty royal family greeted the throngs outside the palace on a balcony shared by the beaming bride, the descendant of coal miners and daughter of run-of-the-mill Brits made good."

Growing Up

Catherine Elizabeth Middleton was born on January 9, 1982 in the Royal Berkshire Hospital in Reading, Berkshire, close to where her family lived in **rural** southern England. She was the first child of Michael and Carole Middleton.

There was little in Catherine's family background to suggest that she would one day marry a future king. Catherine's parents had met through their jobs as flight crew for British Airways, when they worked at nearby Heathrow Airport. The couple bought a house in the village of Bradfield Southend and married in June 1980.

BREAKING BOUNDARIES

THE YOUNG PRINCE

Catherine's birth brought great joy to her family and friends but it was not front-page news. By contrast, the birth of her future husband, and the future king, Prince William Arthur Philip Louis Wales on June 21, 1982 was a huge event. It was greeted by a 41-gun salute and global media coverage.

Prince William was born just a few months after his future wife.

The countryside was a perfect place to bring up a young family. Catherine was soon joined by younger sister Philippa, also known as Pippa, who was born in 1983. Brother James arrived in 1987.

Catherine (right) is pictured with her mother and her sister Pippa.

THEN and NOW

An Ordinary Family

Most people who marry royalty come from privileged or noble families. Catherine's family history is more ordinary. Her great-grandparents lived in a coal-mining village in northeast England. Her father was born in the UK in Leeds, Yorkshire, and was the son of an airline pilot.

Early Childhood

When Catherine was two years old, her father's job took the family to live in Amman, Jordan. Jordan is a country in the Middle East. They spent more than two years in Jordan. While she was there, Kate attended a local English-language nursery school.

After they returned to the south of England in 1986, Carole Middleton decided that the jet-set airline life was not a good fit for the mother of a young family. She started a company called Party Pieces. Its aim was to source party products for children's parties. Catherine and her sister appeared as models in the company's catalogue. The success of Party Pieces would make a big difference to the family's fortunes.

Just your Average Family

Lesley Scutter, a neighbor, remembers Catherine and her family in Claudia Joseph's book *Kate Middleton: A Princess in Waiting*:

"I remember going to parties … and Carole and Mike would be there. They were just a normal family —a really nice couple with well-behaved kids."

Starting School

Catherine and Pippa went to a local Church of England elementary school. Before long, Party Pieces was a success. It meant that the family could afford to send their children to the private and **exclusive** St. Andrew's School, in the nearby town of Pangbourne.

Three-year-old Catherine enjoys the great outdoors on a family vacation.

9

Triumphs and Troubles

School friends remember Catherine as a tall, popular girl who starred in school sports teams and drama productions. But she still had to face the problem of bullying when she moved to a school called Downe House at age 13. Like many teenagers before and since, Catherine discovered that anyone can be the victim of bullies.

Marlborough College

After just two terms at the school, Catherine moved to Marlborough College. Her parents' thriving party business meant they could afford the school's tuition. The family also moved into a big new home.

Catherine was a member of the field hockey team at both St. Andrew's School and Marlborough College.

THEN and NOW

Equal Education

The first girls attended Marlborough College in 1968, which was earlier than most of Britain's traditional **public schools**. Other girls who were educated there include Samantha Cameron, the wife of British Prime Minister David Cameron, and Prince William's cousin Princess Eugenie.

Catherine lived at the boarding school. At first she was homesick and lacked confidence. Catherine hid her unhappiness by working hard at her studies and proving herself on the sports field, particularly in field hockey and tennis. By the time she left Marlborough, Catherine had the courage and the grades she needed to go on to college.

Teen Crush

Catherine denied a story that she had a poster of the young Prince William on her wall as a teenager:

"I had the Levi's guy on my wall, not a picture of William."

Student Days

Before going to college, Catherine decided to take a **gap year.** She had left Marlborough College with a passion for art. The majestic Italian city of Florence was the perfect destination for a young art lover.

Fun in Florence

The city of Florence is home to some of the greatest works of art in the world, from Michelangelo's statue of David to the paintings of Leonardo da Vinci. Catherine spent several months in the city studying Italian at the British Institute. She is an enthusiastic photographer and was captivated by the incredible buildings and art.

Catherine was just one of many wealthy British teenagers who enjoyed Florence's cafés, nightlife, and bars.

THEN and NOW

The Grand Tour

Catherine's gap year trips to Florence and Chile (see below) gave her the chance to experience more of the world. In centuries past, the children of noble and wealthy families would often travel to European cities to explore other peoples' culture and history. This was known as the Grand Tour.

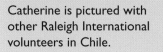

Catherine is pictured with other Raleigh International volunteers in Chile.

Expedition in Chile

After returning from Florence, Catherine went on an expedition in Chile with adventure company Raleigh International. There she helped with community projects and taught English to local children. Amazingly, Prince William had been on the same expedition a few months earlier.

Standing Out from the Crowd

Rachel Humphrys, who looked after volunteers on Catherine's expedition in Chile, remembers her as a special person:

> "She had a certain aura ... and a certain maturity that made her stand out slightly from the other adventurers."

(Source: BBC)

Studying in Scotland

Catherine's gap year gave her time to plan for college. Her excellent exam grades meant she could choose to study almost anywhere. In the end, she chose the University of St. Andrews, in a small historic city on the east coast of Scotland.

By the time Catherine arrived at St. Andrews in September 2001, it had been home to Scotland's oldest university for almost 600 years. However, it was in the news more than ever before because Prince William had chosen to study there. William Wales, as he was known at the university, would study history of art. So, too, would Catherine Middleton.

The university and its students dominate the small city of St. Andrews.

BREAKING BOUNDARIES

COLLEGE QUEEN

When her husband becomes King William, Catherine will be the first British queen, or wife of a king, to have gained a university **degree**.

A New Friend

Catherine and the Prince also lived in the same building when they first arrived at St. Andrews. They became friends and shared stories of their gap year adventures in Chile and their love of sports. In 2002, Prince William famously had a front-row seat when his new friend performed in a charity fashion show.

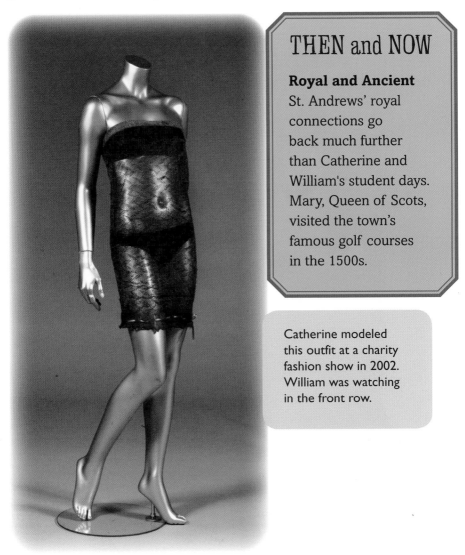

THEN and NOW

Royal and Ancient
St. Andrews' royal connections go back much further than Catherine and William's student days. Mary, Queen of Scots, visited the town's famous golf courses in the 1500s.

Catherine modeled this outfit at a charity fashion show in 2002. William was watching in the front row.

Under the Microscope

Catherine and William became close friends during their first year at college. At one point, William considered leaving St. Andrews but Catherine was one of the people to talk him out of it. In their second year, they moved into a student house with two other friends. The pair said they were still just friends, but the British **tabloid** newspapers began to ask questions.

Attracting Attention

The newspapers were excited to report on the friendship between Catherine and William. In May 2003, *The Sun* newspaper wrote,

"Prince William seemed oblivious to the drama of the rugby game being played in front of him. He had eyes only for the girl beside him —his flatmate and increasingly regular companion Kate Middleton."

Catherine graduated in 2005 with a degree in history of art.

THEN and NOW

Royal Tragedy

William tried hard to protect Catherine from the media's gaze. His mother Diana, Princess of Wales, was one of the world's most photographed women. She died in a car crash while being chased by photographers in 1997. William was just 15 years old.

However, the Royal Family asked the media to leave William alone during his studies. He and Catherine managed to stay out of the newspapers for much of their time at St. Andrews. They also tried to appear in public together as little as possible.

Student Success

Catherine made the most of her time at college. She was cofounder of a group called the Lumsden Club. The women-only club raised money for charity and held social events. It was a rival to an all-male club at the university.

A Working Woman

Only their closest friends know when Catherine's friendship with William turned into romance. In 2004, pictures appeared in the newspapers showing the couple on a skiing vacation with William's father, Prince Charles. The following year, Catherine graduated from university and moved to London. William was training to join the British armed forces.

Catherine appeared in public when William graduated from the Sandhurst Military Academy in December 2006.

Starting a job is difficult for any young **graduate**, but Catherine also had to cope with being followed by journalists and photographers every day. She tried to keep a low profile when working for fashion company Jigsaw and her own family's Party Pieces business.

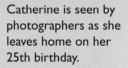

Catherine is seen by photographers as she leaves home on her 25th birthday.

Romance and Rumors

Catherine spent time with William when he was in London. This started the rumor that the couple would soon announce their **engagement**. Then came the news that Catherine would be given her own **security** team, just like a member of the British Royal Family. It had been tough for her, as she hadn't been getting much support to help her deal with the attention of the media.

Media Pressure

Royal photographer Arthur Edwards described the media pressure on Catherine during an official inquiry into the press:

"She has been stopped at traffic lights, where they climb off their motorbikes and start photographing her. She has been out shopping in stores and they run into the stores after her. She uses public transport[ation] a lot—or she did—but they climb on the buses and the bus driver is having to throw them off."

19

Heartbreak

By the beginning of 2007, the media was convinced that Catherine and William would soon be engaged. However, a truly unexpected announcement was then made. Catherine and William had split up.

Pictures of Catherine and William together in early 2007 hinted that all was not well in their relationship.

Catherine was present when William received his "wings" in 2008, which meant he had qualified as a search and rescue pilot.

William had been working full-time as an officer in the British army. His job included long stays away from London. Catherine and William often spent nights out with their friends rather than with each other. Journalists who followed the Royal Family suggested that Catherine had wanted William to commit to their future.

Back for Good

While the press and public tried to work out what had gone wrong, the couple said they were still friends. But within a few weeks they were seen out together. On July 1, 2007, Catherine went to Wembley Stadium in London for a concert in memory of William's mother. By the end of the evening, William and Kate were in each other's arms. It looked like they were back together.

A Joint Decision?

Royal expert Nicholas Witchell tried to explain the break-up of Catherine and William:

"One must suspect, though I don't know that this is absolutely certain, that it is more his decision than hers. He has said in the past that he is too young to get married."

Engaged to a Prince

On November 16, 2010, Catherine and William ended years of rumours and anticipation when they announced that they were to marry. William had proposed during a vacation in Kenya. Catherine described it as being "very romantic."

In the years since their brief split, both had been busy with their careers. Catherine had found it difficult to work in London with so much media attention, so she returned to her family's business. William was committed to being a search and rescue helicopter pilot.

Fact:
The sapphire engagement ring that William gave to Catherine had belonged to his mother, Diana, Princess of Wales.

This official photograph shows Catherine and William on the day they announced their engagement to the world.

Lady Elizabeth Bowes-Lyon had to be asked three times before she agreed to marry Prince Albert in 1923. Her husband was crowned King George VI in 1937.

Out of Her Comfort Zone

During an interview on the day the engagement was announced, Catherine revealed she was worried about joining the Royal Family:

"It's obviously nerve-wracking, because I don't know the ropes really, William is obviously used to it, but I'm willing to learn quickly and work hard."

Rare Interview

The couple gave a television interview at the time of their engagement. Many who saw it realized that they actually knew very little about the woman who would marry the future king. Despite the **relentless** press attention, Catherine, her family, and friends have rarely given interviews.

BREAKING BOUNDARIES

HUMBLE ORIGINS

Throughout her relationship with William, the media focused on Catherine's ordinary family. Usually, the heir to the throne married someone from a royal or aristocratic family. This was the first time a "commoner" has married someone from the royal family since Anne Hyde married the future James II in 1660.

World Famous

The engagement instantly made Catherine famous around the world. Her fiancé had been in the spotlight since the day he was born. He had learned the hard way about the dangers of saying the wrong thing or losing his temper in public. How would Catherine cope with this level of fame?

The royal engagement was big news all around the world.

Many experts were amazed by how easily Catherine adapted to the pressure of being engaged to a future king. This was because when the couple announced their engagement, she already had many years' experience of living her life in public. As well as keeping quiet herself, Catherine's close circle of friends and family did not talk to the media about her private life.

BREAKING BOUNDARIES

BREAKING WITH TRADITION

There are not many families more traditional than the British Royal Family. Some people were shocked that Catherine and William lived together before their marriage. However, this is not unusual for modern couples.

Catherine and William made some public appearances during their engagement, including a visit to a lifeboat station close to William's base in North Wales.

Fashion Sense

In public, Catherine quickly became a fashion icon. The dress she wore in her engagement photos was created by Brazilian-born designer Daniella Helayel, who designs for Issa. Fans of Catherine rushed out to buy the dress. While famous fashion designers want Catherine to be seen in their designs, she also likes to wear clothes from some affordable stores.

"A Down-to-Earth Girl"

A royal **aide** described Catherine's personality:

"What you see in public is what you get in private —very warm, very kind, very thoughtful, sensitive, very down-to-earth, very intelligent."

Learning to Be Royal

Being part of the Royal Family is about more than just handling the media. In the months after her engagement, Catherine had to learn the **complex** rules and customs that the royal household follow.

Catherine had to learn all about the tradition of royal pageants such as the annual Trooping of the Color.

THEN and NOW

Royal Protocol

Royal **protocol** is a series of rules that have developed over hundreds of years. They say how people should act around the Queen and Royal Family. They date from a time when the **monarch** was believed to be chosen by God. Supporters also say these rules avoid embarrassment for anyone meeting royalty.

Media reports before the wedding revealed that Catherine was taking **etiquette** lessons so she would not make any embarrassing slips. She knew that experts would notice if she made mistakes. Catherine had to learn how to greet other royals and foreign leaders, the correct way of shaking hands, and how to curtsey. She was very quick to pick up the rules, which might appear strange and even silly to most ordinary people.

Meet "the Firm"

The British Royal Family is not like any other family. The Queen herself is said to call it "the Firm." Catherine had to fit in with the many different personalities in the family. She is believed to be close to William's stepmother, the Duchess of Cornwall.

Fact:
The Royal Family love to attend horse races and polo events. Catherine has often been seen at these events, despite the fact that she is allergic to horses.

Catherine chats with her future brother-in-law, Prince Harry, during an official royal ceremony at Windsor Castle.

The Royal Wedding

Catherine was not the only person who was awake early on April 29, 2011 to prepare for the big day. Many people had camped overnight outside Buckingham Palace in London to see the royal couple up close.

The wedding in 1,000-year-old Westminster Abbey was shown on video screens for the crowds outside.

10:51 a.m.
Catherine left the hotel where she had stayed overnight with her family.

11:00 a.m.
The bride, her father, and bridesmaids led by sister Pippa arrived at Westminster Abbey where 1,900 guests were waiting. This was the first chance for the crowds to see Catherine's wedding dress, designed by Sarah Burton.

The couple traveled by horse-drawn carriage from Westminster Abbey to Buckingham Palace.

12:09 p.m.
The married couple leave Westminster Abbey, smiling and waving to the crowds.

12:28 p.m.
The couple arrive at Buckingham Palace. They are joined by 600 guests for the wedding reception.

1:27 p.m.
Catherine and William appear on the Palace balcony, where they kiss for the cheering crowds.

The couple later left Buckingham Palace in a vintage car for an evening reception with family and friends. Catherine was now a member of the Royal Family.

The royal wedding was hailed around the world as a boost to the British monarchy and British tourism. Although not entirely paid for by the public, some people complained that too much public money was spent on associated costs, such as security.

Party at the Palace

Catherine's wedding day did not end when she left the reception for a last wave to the crowds. After many of the well-wishers had headed home, the royal couple and 300 guests were back at the Palace. The couple partied with their families and closest friends in the historic throne room.

After the Party

The day after the wedding, newspapers, television, and the Internet were full of details and photos of the wedding. The Duke and Duchess of Cambridge were whisked away by helicopter for a private weekend in a secret British location. A few days later, they headed for a luxury resort on the Indian Ocean islands of the Seychelles to relax after the stress of the wedding.

Fact:
The music at the wedding party included a performance by singer Ellie Goulding. This was followed by the thumping dance music that the couple and their friends often danced to in London's most exclusive nightclubs.

The couple left the wedding reception in a vintage car, which had been decorated in traditional wedding style.

Michael and Carole Middleton could never have predicted that one day they would stand on the balcony of Buckingham Palace with members of the Royal Family.

Catherine may have thought she had been in the spotlight before her big day. However, it was nothing compared with the global attention on the young royals after their fairy-tale wedding.

THEN and NOW

Duke and Duchess

On the day of the wedding, the Royal Family announced that the couple would be given the new titles of the Duke and Duchess of Cambridge. A duke is the title traditionally given to the highest rank of the nobility. In the past, dukes usually controlled a large area of land.

Married Life

The wedding was the perfect start for William and Catherine's married life together. As husband and wife they would have to attend glittering social events or go on foreign tours, but the pair were determined to keep in touch with ordinary life as much as possible.

Catherine would face a life very different from most women. She would not be able to have a normal career because of her royal position. Catherine would have to find a role for herself while supporting her husband, the future king.

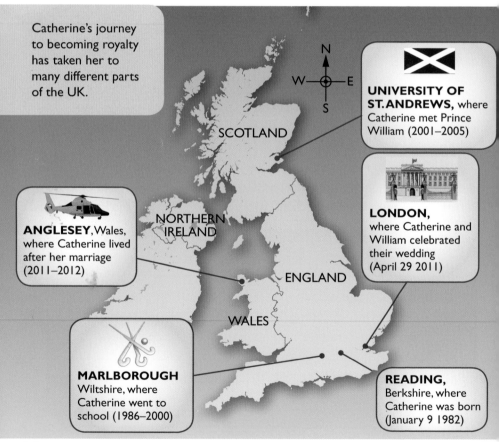

Catherine's journey to becoming royalty has taken her to many different parts of the UK.

UNIVERSITY OF ST. ANDREWS, where Catherine met Prince William (2001–2005)

LONDON, where Catherine and William celebrated their wedding (April 29 2011)

ANGLESEY, Wales, where Catherine lived after her marriage (2011–2012)

MARLBOROUGH Wiltshire, where Catherine went to school (1986–2000)

READING, Berkshire, where Catherine was born (January 9 1982)

SCOTLAND

NORTHERN IRELAND

ENGLAND

WALES

THEN and NOW

Royal Marriages

Catherine's journey from an ordinary family background to become one of the world's most famous women seems like a fairy tale. However, royal couples face many challenges. Three of Queen Elizabeth II's four children have been divorced, including William's parents Prince Charles and Diana, Princess of Wales.

Queen Elizabeth's third child, Prince Andrew, married Sarah Ferguson in 1986. They were divorced in 1996.

Official Duties

In May 2011, Catherine got a taste of the official duties that would become a growing part of her new life. The Duchess joined her husband and the Queen in welcoming the U.S. president, Barack Obama, and his wife, Michelle, to a reception at Buckingham Palace.

Military Wife

Catherine, Duchess of Cambridge, spent much of her first year of marriage far away from the bright lights of London. Her first married home was a rented cottage on the island of Anglesey in North Wales. The Duchess lived the life of a military wife, while William continued his career as a search and rescue pilot.

Just a few days after her wedding, Catherine was spotted doing the weekly shopping at the local supermarket. She was accompanied by several security guards as she loaded the shopping bags into her car.

Catherine lived in a rented cottage in Anglesey after getting married. William was based nearby.

THEN and NOW

Marriage and the Military
Queen Elizabeth II also started her married life as a military wife after her marriage to Prince Philip in 1947. Before she became queen, Princess Elizabeth spent time in Malta while her husband was stationed there as a naval officer.

BREAKING BOUNDARIES

SUPPORTING THE ARMED FORCES

Catherine is well aware of the sacrifices made by military personnel serving overseas. Alongside her husband and his brother Prince Harry, she is **patron** of a foundation that supports military personnel and their families.

Serving Overseas

The Duchess has spoken to other military wives of her fears about the dangers of William's job. In 2012, the Duke was stationed in the Falkland Islands for several weeks. Catherine admitted publicly that she missed William during his time overseas.

While William was on duty, Catherine's black cocker spaniel Lupo kept her company.

Duchess of Cambridge

While William was on duty in the Falkland Islands, Catherine made her first speech as a working royal. Catherine was visiting a **hospice** for sick children. It was one of the main charities she had chosen to support. Charity work is a major part of the Duchess's public life.

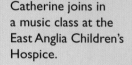

Catherine joins in a music class at the East Anglia Children's Hospice.

THEN and NOW

Supporting Charities

Members of the British Royal Family have been connected to charities and organizations since the 1700s. Today, the Queen and her family are patrons of more than 3,000 organizations. Royal involvement can help the charities to gain publicity and raise money for their cause.

Charity Work

Catherine's choice of charities shows her concerns as a public figure. Action on Addiction works with children and families affected by drug and alcohol addiction. The Duchess's love of children was shown by her support for the East Anglia Children's Hospice for sick children.

Catherine supports the Art Room, which uses art to build children's confidence and self-esteem. This reflects her deep interest and love of art. Catherine also became a patron of the National Portrait Gallery, in London.

During a visit to the Art Room, in Oxford, UK, Catherine admires the work of a young artist.

A Princess of the People

Graham Butland of the East Anglia Children's Hospice, of which Catherine is patron, praised her on how well she deals with her fans:

"She was absolutely magnificent with the children and families, she seems to have the ability to just drop into a group of people and immediately be able to establish a **rapport**."

Overseas Tours

While Catherine spent much of the first year of her marriage living quietly, she also had official duties to carry out. The Duke and Duchess made their first overseas tour to Canada, where the Queen is head of state, a few weeks after their marriage. The Duchess was greeted by cheering crowds. In 2012, the couple traveled to Malaysia, Singapore, the Solomon Islands, and Tuvalu as part of the celebrations for Queen Elizabeth's Diamond Jubilee.

Fact:
The Diamond Jubilee celebrated 60 years of Queen Elizabeth II being on the throne. There were special events, concerts, parades, and parties throughout the year.

The Duchess of Cambridge has to be as comfortable meeting world leaders, such as U.S. President Barack Obama, as she is meeting ordinary people.

Catherine showed her love of sports when cheering on Great Britain's athletes at the London Olympics in 2012.

As part of her royal duties, Catherine has often traveled with the Queen and other members of the Royal Family to events around the UK.

Media Trouble

Catherine tries to avoid the limelight when not "on duty." The publication of photographs of the Duchess sunbathing on vacation in 2012 were a reminder that the media is always watching.

Life Through a Lens

A royal aide spoke of his thoughts on media intrusion:

"It's hard to think where they could have gone that is more secluded in Europe, and yet even there a photographer was concealed over a long period of time, photographing them through a long lens and watching their every move, and for that reason, this was just a step too far."

Mother of a Monarch

Catherine had only just gotten used to being married to a future monarch when the Royal Family announced some exciting news. Catherine was expecting a baby in July 2013. The baby would be third in line to the throne from the day he or she is born.

The news that Catherine was expecting a baby brought her even more attention, as she continued her charity work in 2013.

THEN and NOW

Rules of Succession
For hundreds of years, the British crown has passed to the oldest male child when the previous monarch dies. A woman could only become queen if, like Queen Elizabeth II, she had no brothers. In 2013, this ancient law was changed so that the eldest son or daughter of the Duke and Duchess would be next in line to the throne after William himself.

The pregnancy was not easy and, early on, Catherine spent several days in hospital because of morning sickness. Even here, the couple faced problems with the media, when a radio prank went badly wrong. The nurse Jacintha Saldanha tragically took her own life after mistakenly giving details of the Duchess's health to two Australian DJs pretending to be members of the Royal Family.

The day when the royal baby was due to be born was a closely guarded secret. On July 22, 2013, news spread around the world that Catherine had been taken to the hospital. The world's media camped outside an exclusive hospital in London, desperate for any news on the future monarch.

Finally, it was announced. At 4:24 p.m., Catherine had given birth to a son. The baby would be called Prince George. As she introduced her son to waiting crowds the following day, Catherine said she was "very emotional" about becoming a mother.

A Fairy-Tale Princess?

Like so many girls, the young Catherine Middleton must have dreamed of one day marrying a handsome prince and becoming the mother of a future monarch. Unlike most people, Catherine's dreams have come true. But is royal life really as magical as it appears from the outside?

The Drawbacks

Being a member of the Royal Family certainly has drawbacks. The Royal Family have to be careful not to get involved in political issues. This means they are often not able to say what they think. Catherine has to deal with constant media attention on her clothes, family, and every other aspect of her life. Even when she is out of the public eye, privacy is difficult to find in a household crowded with officials and aides.

Catherine can learn much about how to remain popular from her husband's grandmother, Queen Elizabeth II.

Many people think that Catherine's informal style is well suited to the life of a 21st-century princess.

Of course, the wealth, fame, and privilege of royal life make up for some of these drawbacks. In the past, royal marriages have often been arranged between noble families. Catherine and her husband have chosen each other. This, along with her huge public popularity, will help to protect Catherine from the stresses of royal life.

BREAKING BOUNDARIES

SAVING THE ROYAL FAMILY?

For many people in Britain and around the world, the monarchy seems hopelessly out of date. Surely leaders should be chosen by their people, not born to rule? Royalists hope that Catherine and William's more informal style makes them more appealing to younger generations and will help to **preserve** the image, and ensure the future, of the Royal Family.

Glossary

aide assistant or helper (to someone important, such as someone in the Royal Family)

complex difficult to understand because there are many parts

coronation ceremony when a person is crowned and becomes king or queen

degree qualification given by a university to somebody after three or more years of studying there

engagement when two people have agreed to get married but before they are actually married

etiquette code of polite behavior in society or among members of a particular profession or group

exclusive something, such as a club, which excludes some people, either because it is very expensive or has rules about who can join

fiancé man engaged to be married (an engaged woman is a fiancée)

gap year year between leaving school and going to college, which is often used for traveling or working abroad

graduate describing a person who has a degree. When they complete a degree, they have graduated.

hospice place where very ill or dying people are cared for

media name for all means of communication, such as television, radio, newspapers, and online information

monarch someone who rules over a country without being elected, such as a king or a queen

patron leading supporter of a charity or some other cause

preserve keep in good condition

propel push or move something, often with a lot of force

protocol official rule of behavior followed by an organization or group of people

public school in Britain, this phrase actually means a private school where pupils have to pay fees to attend

rapport good or friendly relationship. Sometimes this describes conversation.

relentless never-ending or constant (something without a break)

rural describes something in the countryside. This is opposed to urban, which describes something in the city.

security safety or protection. A well-known person might have security guards

tabloid newspaper that usually contains short and sensational stories, often about celebrities

Timeline

1982   Catherine Elizabeth Middleton is born in Reading, Berkshire, on January 9, the first child of Michael and Carole Middleton

1984   Middleton family moves to Amman, Jordan for two years

1986   Catherine starts attending St. Andrew's School in Pangbourne, Berkshire

2000   Catherine leaves Marlborough College, Wiltshire with A-level qualifications in biology, chemistry, and art

2001   Catherine attends the University of St. Andrews, where she meets Prince William

2005   Catherine graduates from St. Andrews with a degree in the history of art and moves to London

2007   In April, Catherine and William reveal that they have split up, although they are back together again within a few months

2010   Catherine and William announce their engagement in November

2011   Wedding of Catherine Middleton and Prince William in Westminster Abbey on April 29

       The royal couple are greeted warmly on their first official overseas tour of Canada in July

2012   The Royal Family announces that Catherine is expecting a child, after she is admitted to the hospital with morning sickness

2013   The birth of the Duke and Duchess of Cambridge's first child, Prince George, on July 22

Find Out More

Books
Bingham, Jane. *William and Kate: A Royal Love Story*. Chicago: Raintree, 2011.

Doeden, Matt. *Prince William & Kate: A Royal Romance*. Minneapolis, MN: Lerner, 2011.

Mattern, Joanne. *Princess Diana*. New York City: DK, 2006.

Web Sites
www.dukeandduchessofcambridge.org
Catherine and her husband have their own official web site, which is a great place to find the latest news about them.

www.royal.gov.uk/thecurrentroyalfamily/theduchessofcambridge/ theduchessofcambridge.aspx
The official web site of the Royal Family includes profiles of many members of the family, including the Duchess of Cambridge.

www.royalfoundation.com
Find out about the work of the Royal Foundation set up by the Duke and Duchess of Cambridge and Prince Harry.

www.youtube.com/watch?v=DD1Go3NHQXM
Watch the joint interview that Catherine and Prince William gave when they announced their engagement in 2011.

Further Research
If you enjoyed this book and want to learn more about Catherine and the monarchy, try researching some of the following questions:
- Find out more about the charities that Catherine supports and the work that they do. Why do you think she has chosen to support them?
- Catherine is often compared to William's mother Diana, Princess of Wales. Why is this?
- Discover more about the British monarchy and its traditions. Is monarchy still a sensible way to govern a country in a modern world?

Index